Stories of *Titanic's* CHILDREN

BY PEGGY CARAVANTES

Published by The Child's World®
1980 Lookout Drive • Mankato, MN 56003-1705
800-599-READ • www.childsworld.com

Acknowledgments
The Child's World®: Mary Berendes, Publishing Director
Red Line Editorial: Design, editorial direction, and production
Photographs ©: Underwood & Underwood/Corbis, cover, 1; AP Images, 4; Henry
Aldridge and Son/Press Association/AP Images, 7; Hulton-Deutsch Collection/Corbis,
8; Shutterstock Images, 11; Matthew Polak/Sygma/Corbis, 12; Bain Collection/Library
of Congress, 15; Daily Mirror/Mirrorpix/Corbis, 16; Bettmann/Corbis, 18; Bain News
Service/Library of Congress, 21

ISBN 9781634074643

LCCN 2015946308

Printed in the United States of America
Mankato, MN
December, 2015
PA02287

ABOUT THE AUTHOR

After a career in education, Peggy Caravantes fulfilled a lifetime dream to
write. She is the author of numerous children's history books and middle
grade/young adult biographies. Caravantes holds a bachelor of arts degree
in English and a master of educational administration degree. She lives in
San Antonio, Texas.

Table of
CONTENTS

Chapter 1

THE CHILDREN ON THE *TITANIC*

Gleaming stars twinkled in the dark night on April 14, 1912. They set the sky apart from the black waters of the Atlantic Ocean. The *Titanic*, the world's largest ship, was sailing from England to New York. The captain and his crew hoped to prove their ship could make the fastest time on an ocean voyage across the Atlantic.

Despite the speed of the ship, the night was quiet on board. Most of the 115 children on the **liner** had gone to bed. Their noisy activity no longer filled the decks. Six-year-old Douglas Spedden, the son of a wealthy New York family, was staying in one of the first-class **cabins** with his parents. The family was going home after a vacation in Europe.

In the evening, Douglas's nanny had tucked him into bed. She placed Polar, his favorite white teddy bear, beside him. Douglas was tired. During the day, he had been running around and spinning his top on the A Deck. Earlier that morning, his mother, Daisy, had taken him to another deck to play ball. Now he slept soundly.

Lillian Asplund was five years old. She was traveling with her family in the cheaper third-class part of the ship. Lillian hated the odor of their room, which had just been painted. The Asplunds were returning to the United States. They had been living in Sweden with Lillian's grandmother. Lillian's father, mother, and her four brothers also made the trip. One brother was Lillian's twin Carl. The Asplund children were five of the 84 children in the third-class area.

Families with children were housed toward the back of the ship. The cabins were small but neat. Several general areas provided more space for passengers to gather and talk.

The second-class decks were between the fancy first-class and the simpler third-class decks. The children there had also gone to bed for the night. Eight-year-old Marjorie Collyer's family was moving to the United States. They wanted to live in a better climate for her mother's health. The Collyers planned to settle in Idaho and start a fruit farm.

Seven-year-old Eva Hart's family was moving to Canada. Her father hoped to open a business there. Eva had spent all day with her father, whom she adored. While he read his newspaper, she ran her fingers through his wavy dark hair. She had enjoyed breakfast and lunch with both parents that Friday. Eva had also become friends with a bulldog on the ship. She played with it whenever she could. Her father promised her a dog when they settled in Canada. That night, Eva quickly went to sleep.

In a nearby second-class room, eight-year-old Marshall Drew rested on his bunk. He was traveling with his aunt and uncle. Five days earlier, the family had completed a visit to Marshall's grandmother. Before the *Titanic* sailed, Marshall and his father toured the ship. They went into the ship's barbershop. There,

▲ **On April 14, 1912, Eva Hart and her mother wrote a letter together.**

souvenirs of all kinds were sold. Marshall's father bought him a ribbon that said "RMS *Titanic*."

After the *Titanic* set sail, Marshall explored the ship by himself. Sometimes he got lost. But he always found his way back to his aunt and uncle. That night, he was resting but not yet asleep.

At 11:40 p.m., the lives of these children changed forever. The *Titanic* hit an iceberg, tearing the ship's **hull**. The ship began to flood with water. As the ship slowly sank, parents rushed to find places for their children in the lifeboats. There were not enough places for everyone. Many children were separated from family members. A day of fun and games had turned into a night of horror.

Chapter 2

A NIGHT OF TERROR

A loud thump woke young Douglas Spedden. His nanny quickly dressed him. She told him they were going to look at the stars. The Speddens went to the **starboard** side of the ship, where the crew was loading people onto lifeboats. Most passengers were calm. They did not yet realize the dangers they faced.

Douglas, his mother, and his nanny were placed in Lifeboat #3. Crew members cried,

◄ Lifeboats were tied to the upper decks of the *Titanic*.

"Women and children first!" However, Lifeboat #3 was not full. Douglas's father and 20 other men were given places in the boat.

The lifeboat moved through loose ice away from the *Titanic*. It was very cold, and the Spedden family huddled together. Douglas did not seem afraid. He fell asleep on his nanny's lap. When he awoke at dawn, colorful icebergs surrounded them. A sleepy-eyed Douglas told his nanny, "Oh, Muddie, look at the beautiful North Pole with no Santa Claus on it."[1]

In his second-class cabin, Marshall Drew was not quite asleep when the crash occurred. His aunt told him they needed to go on the deck. Marshall took his *Titanic* ribbon with him. Years later, he remembered that night: "It was very cold and the water was calm . . . . The sky was black and the water was black so that you couldn't see any difference between them—it was totally black."[2]

Marshall and his aunt were placed in Lifeboat #11. It was so full that people had to stand up. Marshall's uncle stayed behind. The lifeboat was lowered from the *Titanic* to the water. It moved in jerks. Sometimes the bow, or front of the boat, was up. Sometimes the stern, or back, was up. Marshall feared he and the other passengers would be dumped into the sea. But soon, the lifeboat settled on the ocean waters. Marshall fell asleep.

Back on the *Titanic*, most people in third class had heard the jar of the collision. Water began to creep into the rooms. Passengers peered through **portholes** to see what was happening. Lillian Asplund's father helped her to the deck. Getting there was not easy. Closed doors and narrow stairs slowed their progress. Mr. Asplund helped Lillian into Lifeboat #15.

But Lillian's mother refused to get in. She did not want to leave her husband and sons. Mr. Asplund told her, "Go ahead. We will get into one of the other boats."[3] She held on to her youngest child, Felix, and they joined Lillian in the lifeboat. Lifeboat #15 was the last lifeboat to leave the starboard side of the ship. As the boat was lowered, Lillian could see her father. He was holding her twin Carl in his arms. Her two older brothers stood on each side of him. She never saw any of them again.

Marjorie Collyer's mother later described the collision she felt in their second-class cabin. "It was as if the ship had been seized by a giant hand, shaken once, twice; then stopped dead at its course," she said.[4] Marjorie's father brought her to the deck where Lifeboat #14 was being loaded. Mrs. Collyer refused to leave her husband. A sailor thrust Marjorie into the boat.

Mr. Collyer shouted to his wife, "Go, Lotty! Be brave and go! I'll get a seat in another boat."[5] Finally, Mrs. Collyer entered

▲ **Passengers on the *Titanic* could look out through the porthole windows.**

the lifeboat. Marjorie did not know that she would never see her father again. She later remembered, "I cried hardest when I thought of my dolly back there in the water with nobody to mind it and keep it from getting wet."[6]

When the *Titanic* hit the iceberg, Eva Hart was sound asleep. To Eva's mother, it felt like a minor bump. But she still insisted that Mr. Hart go check on it. When he came back, his face was pale. He led Eva and her mother to Lifeboat #14. He waved goodbye and turned to help others onto the boat. Steam hissing from the sinking ship scared Eva. She screamed for her father. Soon, she could no longer see him.

Chapter 3

THE JOURNEY AND RESCUE

Children and adults had some of the same experiences on the water. As the lifeboats were lowered as much as 70 feet (21 m) into the water, distress rockets shot into the sky. These signals were the *Titanic*'s only hope for rescue. Crew members on each lifeboat, sometimes aided by adult passengers, rowed away from the sinking ship. Shouts echoed from lifeboat to lifeboat.

Officer Harold Lowe in Lifeboat #14 decided to tie together several of the boats. He wanted to keep them from getting lost in the dark. He moved all of his #14 passengers to the other boats. He planned to go back for more people. As people were shuffled between boats, Eva Hart was separated from her mother. For a while, she feared she had lost both parents.

The *Titanic* remained afloat for about two hours after the crash. Then the people in the lifeboats watched as the great ship slipped slowly below the water's surface. First, the bow went down. Row after row of porthole lights disappeared. Finally, the stern stood straight up before it plunged into the black sea. It was 2:20 a.m. The sinking ship threw hundreds of people into the cold black waters, yelling and crying. The terrible sounds of these passengers struggling in the water became one long moan. Then the sea became silent.

By dawn, the wind had increased, making the sea choppy. The situation was dangerous. Passengers in the lifeboats had no water, no food, and no **compass** to guide them. The people in Lifeboat #8 saw a light to the north. For a while, they rowed toward it. They hoped it was a rescue ship. But the light never got any closer to them.

Finally, another light could be seen in the distance. It was a ship. Passengers made crude torches so that people on the ship could see them. They set fire to a newspaper in one boat and to a straw hat in another. The small fires provided a little light. But they could not protect passengers from the bitter cold. Some women shared extra coats and shawls with others.

As the RMS *Carpathia* neared the lifeboats, rough seas made it hard for the boats to get close to the bigger ship. They bounced off the **keel**. Sailors made rope ladders to pull the people onto the ship.

The sailors used burlap mailbags to haul the children aboard. This frightened many of them. But Marshall Drew recalled, "I thought it was a pretty good ride until a sailor dumped me out on the deck."[7] Passengers on the *Carpathia* provided food and blankets for the *Titanic* survivors. Soon, news spread that the *Carpathia* was bringing the *Titanic* survivors to New York. As the rescue ship anchored, the docks were packed with people. Crew members tried to keep track of the names of more than 700 rescued passengers as they left the *Carpathia*.

The crew of the RMS *Carpathia* found and rescued survivors ▶ from the *Titanic*.

In the confusion, no one asked Marshall Drew his name. He was left off of the first list of survivors. His father thought he was dead. When Mr. Drew finally found Marshall, he kept saying, "Are you sure you are my boy?"[8] Later that day, Marshall's aunt left him at a hotel while she shopped for new clothing. She figured he would entertain himself by drawing.

Marshall found a sheet of paper and a small knife in a desk drawer. He punched holes in the paper in the shape of a sinking ship. A reporter for the *New York World* was looking for *Titanic* survivors. He noticed Marshall sitting in the lobby and went over to talk to him. After seeing the boy's drawing, the reporter took a picture of him. The next day, Marshall's photograph appeared in the newspaper.

Marjorie Collyer was also interviewed when she arrived in New York. The *Brooklyn Eagle* published a picture of her clasping Eleanor, her new doll. Eleanor was a gift from other children who had heard about her experience. The doll helped comfort Marjorie after she lost her father.

◄ **Marjory, a girl on the RMS *Carpathia*, shared her blankets and clothing with children from the *Titanic*.**

Chapter 4

MANY YEARS LATER

After the *Carpathia* reached New York, most of the children returned to their families. Many had fathers or mothers who had died in the sinking ship. Often, the children had painful memories of what happened. But they were lucky to survive. When the ship sank, 1,517 people died. Only about half of the children on the ship survived.

Marshall Drew settled in Waverly, Rhode Island. He became a teacher and an artist. He knew that his life could have been cut short by the *Titanic* disaster. He always said, "Let that be a lesson to you—enjoy each day that you have."[9]

Eva Hart had been in the last lifeboat rescued by the *Carpathia*. Once in New York, she discovered that her father had died. She and her mother decided that there was no reason to continue on to Canada. They returned to England. Later in life, she had several jobs: singer, politician, and English magistrate, or judge. She did not like to talk about the *Titanic*, perhaps because of the nightmares she had for many years. In 1993, she finally spoke about watching the ship sink. She said, "I never closed my eyes. I didn't sleep at all. I saw it, I heard it, and nobody could possibly forget it."[10] Hart died three years later, at the age of 91.

Lillian Asplund was the last of the *Titanic* survivors with any memory of the incident. The remaining two survivors were infants when they were on the ship. Lillian died at age 99. She worked as a secretary for most of her life. She avoided talking about the *Titanic*, hating to recall the great loss of her father and three brothers.

Marjorie Collyer and her mother struggled in New York. They had no money or place to live. The American Red Cross helped them get to Idaho, the place where Mr. Collyer had been headed. It was too lonely without him, so Marjorie and her mother returned to England. Some friends collected money to assist with their tickets. As an adult, Marjorie often thought about her time on the *Titanic*, and she missed her father. "Life can be very unkind," she wrote.[11]

Douglas Spedden became known worldwide for a photograph of him spinning his top on the *Titanic*. After he returned home, his mother wrote a book for him. The book told how Douglas's favorite teddy bear survived the journey on the *Titanic*. Decades later, a relative found the book and published it. The book was called *Polar, the Titanic Bear*.

After its sinking, the ruins of the *Titanic* were lost. In 1985, Dr. Robert Ballard and his research team discovered the wreck. This discovery brought back to the survivors memories of the great tragedy.

Marjorie Collyer and her mother arrived in New York ▶ after they were rescued.

GLOSSARY

cabins (KA-binz): Cabins are rooms where passengers stay and sleep on a ship. Families on the *Titanic* stayed in cabins.

compass (KUHM-pus): A compass is an instrument that shows direction. Without a compass, *Titanic* survivors struggled to locate rescue ships.

hull (HUL): A hull is the rigid frame and outer shell of a ship. The hull of the *Titanic* scraped against an iceberg.

keel (KEYL): A keel is a strong metal beam that runs the length of a ship and serves as the ship's backbone. Damage to the keel will cause a ship to lean to one side.

liner (LI-nur): A liner is a commercial ship carrying passengers on a regular route. At the time it was built, the *Titanic* was the largest liner in the world.

portholes (PORT-holz): Portholes are small circular windows in a ship's side. On the *Titanic*, the portholes helped light the lower areas of the ship.

souvenirs (su-veh-NEERS): Souvenirs are objects that people keep as reminders of a place or event. Passengers bought souvenirs in a shop on the *Titanic*.

starboard (STAR-bord): The starboard side is the right side when a person is facing the front of a ship from the inside. Some lifeboats were held on the starboard side of the ship.

SOURCE NOTES

1. Walter Lord. *A Night to Remember*. New York: Henry Holt and Company, 1955. Print. 148.

2. Jackie Sheckler Finch. "Tale of a Titanic Survivor." *Examiner*. Examiner.com Entertainment, 15 April 2012. Web. 25 May 2015.

3. "Last US Titanic Survivor Is Dead." *BBC News*. BBC, 7 May 2006. Web. 20 May 2015.

4. Judith Geller. *Titanic: Women and Children First*. New York: W.W. Norton, 1998. Print. 118.

5. Ibid. 117–118.

6. Ibid.

7. Jackie Sheckler Finch. "Tale of a Titanic Survivor." *Examiner*. Examiner.com Entertainment, 15 April 2012. Web. 25 May 2015.

8. Richard Davenport-Hines. *Voyagers of the Titanic*. New York: William Morrow, 2012. Print. 287.

9. Jackie Scheckler Finch. "Tale of a Titanic Survivor." *Examiner*. Examiner.com Entertainment, 15 April 2012. Web. 25 May 2015.

10. "Titanic Survivor Dies at 91." *RMS Titanic: 100 Years Later*. New York Times Service, n.d. Web. 20 May 2015.

11. Judith Geller. *Titanic: Women and Children First*. New York: W.W. Norton, 1998. Print. 119–121.

TO LEARN MORE

Books

Adams, Simon. *Titanic*. New York: DK Publishing, 2009.

Fullman, Joe. *The Story of Titanic for Children*. London: Carlton, 2015.

Hopkinson, Deborah. *Titanic: Voices from the Disaster*. New York: Scholastic, 2014.

Stewart, Melissa. *Titanic*. Washington, DC: National Geographic Society, 2012.

Web Sites

Visit our Web site for links about the *Titanic*'s children:

childsworld.com/links

Note to Parents, Teachers, and Librarians: We routinely verify our Web links to make sure they are safe and active sites. So encourage your readers to check them out!

INDEX